All About

TRADING IN THE INDUS VALLEY

Brenda and Brian Williams

Raintree

Raintree is an imprint of Capstone Global Library Limited, a company incorporated in England and Wales having its registered office at 7 Pilgrim Street, London, EC4V 6LB – Registered company number: 6695582

www.raintreepublishers.co.uk
myorders@raintreepublishers.co.uk

First published in 2008 as Trading Up: Indus Valley Trade

Editorial: Louise Galpine and Claire Throp
Design: Richard Parker and Tinstar Design (www.tinstar.co.uk)
Illustrations: International Mapping
Picture Research: Mica Brancic
Production: Victoria Fitzgerald

Originated by Capstone Global Library Ltd
Printed and bound in China by CTPS

ISBN 978 1 406 28579 6 (hardback)
18 17 16 15 14
10 9 8 7 6 5 4 3 2 1

British Library Cataloguing in Publication Data
A full catalogue record for this book is available from the British Library.

Acknowledgements
We would like to thank the following for permission to reproduce photographs: AKG-images p. 22; Alamy pp. 10–11, 24–25 (Mike Goldwater); Ancient Art & Architecture Collection Ltd. p. 16; Art Resource p. 6; Art Resource NY/Scala p. 24; Corbis pp. 5 (Lowell Georgia), 7 (Diego Lezama Orezzoli), 9, 19 (Angelo Hornak), 21 (Ric Ergenbright), 23 (Charles E Rotkin); Corbis/The Art Archive p. 20; Robert Harding pp. 27 (Paolo Koch), 13 (Luca Tettoni); TopFoto pp. 17, 26; TopFoto/Ancient Art & Architecture Collection Ltd p. 12; www.mohenjodaro.net p. 15.

Cover photograph of seals from Mohenjo-daro, Pakistan, reproduced with permission of Robert Harding World Imagery.

We would like to thank Nancy Harris and Asko Parpola for their invaluable help in the preparation of this book.

Contents

Some words are printed in bold, **like this**. You can find out what they mean on page 30. You can also look in the box at the bottom of the page where they first appear.

Welcome to the dig

A team of people is exploring a special place. These people are called **archaeologists**. Archaeologists dig in the ground. They do this to find out about people who lived a long time ago. They have found bricks in this city. The bricks are 4,000 years old.

The city of Mohenjo-daro is near the Indus River in Asia (see map below). The Indus people also lived in smaller towns by rivers.

This map shows you where Mohenjo-daro was. It also shows another city, Harappa.

archaeologist person who digs in the ground to find out about the past
trader person who buys and sells things

Archaeologists are history detectives. They dig for clues.

We learned about the Indus people from clues they left behind. Archaeologists have dug up things that show some Indus people were **traders**. Traders buy and sell things.

An amazing find

Explorers found the **ruins** of Harappa in the 1800s. Ruins are the remains of a building or town. They were puzzled when they found stone **seals**. Seals are a kind of stamp. No one could read the writing on the seals.

R. D. Banerji was an Indian **archaeologist**. He discovered Mohenjo-daro in the early 1920s. Seals were found at Mohenjo-daro, too. This meant both cities were built by the same people.

At Mohenjo-daro, archaeologists found walls and streets. They found brick houses and rubbish pits. They uncovered wells (for water). This was once a city.

The archaeologists knew **traders** used seals. They came to buy and sell things. But how did they get there?

Trading fact!

It can be very hot in the Indus Valley. It can get up to 41°C (105°F). People get thirsty. Indus traders carried water in bags made from animal skins.

ruins remains of a building or town
seal kind of stamp

Archaeologists dig away the soil. The deeper they dig, the further back in time they go. This street in Mohenjo-daro was uncovered by archaeologists.

Setting off

Traders set off from farm villages beside the river. They were going to buy and sell things in other places. Before leaving home, they ate a farewell meal. There was plenty to eat. There was bread and fish. Traders also ate peas, melons, and dates. The family prayed to the gods for a safe journey. They would not see the trader again for months.

Indus people did not use money. They traded by swapping things. They might have swapped some fruit for some bread.

Choose your cart

Diggers have found models of three types of Indus cart:

1. Two wheels, with an open top.
2. Two wheels, with a closed top.
3. Four wheels – good for heavy loads.

ox animal of the cattle family, used for pulling ploughs and carts

precious stones stones that are colourful and worth a lot of money

People made clay models of ox carts. Ox carts are still used in India and Pakistan.

Many traders walked. Other traders drove wooden carts. An **ox** pulled the cart. Carts carried **precious stones**. These are stones used to make jewellery. Traders carried timber (wood). They carried a type of metal called copper. They also took food to the city.

Travel from village to village

Some **traders** travelled in boats along the river. This was quicker than walking. But there were sometimes storms and floods.

Going by cart was dangerous, too. There were tigers and snakes. There were no good roads. The traders walked along dusty tracks. They were glad to reach the next village.

In the villages the traders could rest. They drank cool water from the village well. Traders met friends and passed on news.

Going south, the river moved boats along. Going north was harder. Boats went against the water flow. The Indus people would have travelled in boats like the one in the picture.

The big city

Traders saw Mohenjo-daro from far off. The city had a wall 6 metres (20 feet) high. No enemy could get in. Gate guards checked new arrivals. They looked to see what **goods** (things) people carried. They checked what they had to sell.

The city's main street was wide. Two carts could pass on it. Small streets led off the main road. They had rows of houses made of **mud brick**.

To get water, people lowered buckets on ropes into wells. ↓

ceremony special public acts, such as worship of a god or honouring a ruler
goods things people make and sell
mud brick brick made from wet dirt, often mixed with straw

This is the Great Bath. All the water has gone from it. The pool was made of bricks. They were painted with tar. This meant that no water leaked out of the cracks.

Mohenjo-daro was a clean city. Dirty water from houses emptied into drains under the street. Dustmen took away rubbish.

The city had about 700 wells. Water was important. The Great Bath had a big pool. People may have bathed there as part of a religious **ceremony**. A ceremony was a special act to worship a god.

Sleeping on the roof

Traders could stay in hotels in the city. Remains of buildings with lots of small rooms have been found. These buildings also seem to have bathrooms. They may have been hotels.

Traders sometimes stayed with friends. Some homes had only one room. Others had 20 rooms. Most families had a bathroom in their house. In the bathroom there was often a toilet.

Doors and windows were at the back. This kept out noise and dust from the street. Windows had **shutters**. Shutters helped keep out the heat. When it was very hot, people slept outside on the roof at night.

Trading fact!

Cleaners climbed down into the drains through holes. They dug out solid waste from "soak-pits". What a smelly job!

shutters small wooden doors over windows

This is an Indus city toilet. It was flushed by water. Most homes had one.

Checking in

Indus people liked things to be neat. Bricks and pots were often the same size. Roads were straight. City rulers checked **traders** in and out of the city. Traders may have paid **taxes**. Taxes are payments people pay to their rulers.

The building called the "granary" was probably used by traders. The name means "food store". But no grain has been found there.

hieroglyphics writing of ancient Egypt
taxes money or goods paid to rulers

This seal has writing on it. It is hard to work out what it means.

The "granary" was where traders may have weighed their goods. City officials used scales with weights. Traders might also have been paid for their goods here. Traders were paid in food.

Mystery writing

Experts have looked at 2,000 bits of writing on **seals**. They cannot read it. It would help to find the same text written in Indus and in a language we can read. That is how experts first read ancient Egypt's **hieroglyphics** (picture-writing).

Around the workshops

Many people lived in Mohenjo-daro. The rulers (leaders) probably lived in the district now called High Mound. Other people lived in Lower Town.

Lower Town had workshops. People made tools and **weapons**. They made beads and pottery. They made clothes out of cotton.

Traders brought **raw materials** into the city. Raw materials are things such as metal and wood. They are things we can use to make other things. People in the workshops used these materials. For example, they used dried goat **dung** (poo). They put it in the oven with their pots. This made the pots a darker colour.

The "dancing girl"

The "dancing girl" is a **statue** made of a metal called bronze. She wears bangles and beads. **Archaeologists** found other statues of people wearing beads.

dung waste made by animals
raw material wood, stone, clay – anything we use to make something else
statue model of people or animals
weapon tool for killing people in war

This is a cooking pot. It was used by the Indus people.

Ask the gods

A small stone **statue** was found in the Indus Valley. It shows the head of a bearded man. He wears a headband and a cloak. Is he a ruler? No one knows. He may have been a **priest**. A priest leads people in religious worship.

This stone head was found in 1927. Some people called it a "priest-king".

Hindu someone who believes in Hinduism
priest someone who leads people in religious worship
temple building for religious worship

*People may have bathed in the River Indus for religious reasons. Modern **Hindus** in India bathe in the River Ganges. They believe it is a holy river.*

Different animals were shown on **seals**. Were they magic signs? No one knows for certain. Seals like this are found in **temples**. A temple is a building where people say prayers. **Traders** may have prayed for a safe trip.

A circle of rocks puzzled experts for many years. Then local people showed them a special place, made for a god. It was like the ancient Indus rock circle.

Seal the deal

The picture on a **trader's seal** was like a badge. The seal was used like an ink stamp. It made a print when pressed into soft clay. When the clay dried it could be fixed on a sack or basket. It was like a label. Seals were used when making deals.

Indus seals are squares. Their sides are between 2 and 3 centimetres (0.8 and 1.2 inches) long.

This is a zebu bull. These humped cattle live in India today.

What seals show

Some seals have pictures of rhinos, tigers, or elephants. Others show gods.

The most common animal shown on seals is the one-horned bull. It may have been the badge of the richest family. Another seal shows a bull with a hump.

When deals were done, traders packed up to leave. Some loaded their carts. They headed back north. Others went to the port. They went off by ship, to another land.

Set sail

The Indus people lived close to rivers. We know from bone remains that they ate fish. They travelled long distances. We know this because their **seals** have been found in lands far away.

Workers built wooden sailing ships. **Traders** travelled in the ships. They had **goods** to sell overseas. They carried wooden tables and bead necklaces. They even carried pet monkeys.

The Indus Valley people had a good life. It seemed it could last for ever. But it didn't.

Trading fact!

A king in ancient Iraq (see the map on page 4) wrote about the people who came to his kingdom. He said traders from Meluhha came. Experts think he meant the Indus people.

Indus traders travelled along the River Indus. A boat could carry more trade goods than an ***ox*** *cart.*

Mystery ending

Some time after 2000 BC, things went wrong in Mohenjo-daro. It became dirty. People stopped looking after drains and wells. Did enemies attack? **Archaeologists** have found no signs of battles. The city may have become too crowded. Perhaps floods drove people there from their villages.

*Fourteen skeletons were found in one room. It is possible that people were not given **funerals** because the city was in such bad trouble. A funeral is a way to say goodbye to a dead person.*

civilization way of life that is highly developed
funeral ceremony for a dead person

Trading fact!

Archaeologists found hidden jewels in Mohenjo-daro. Had their owners hidden them and run away?

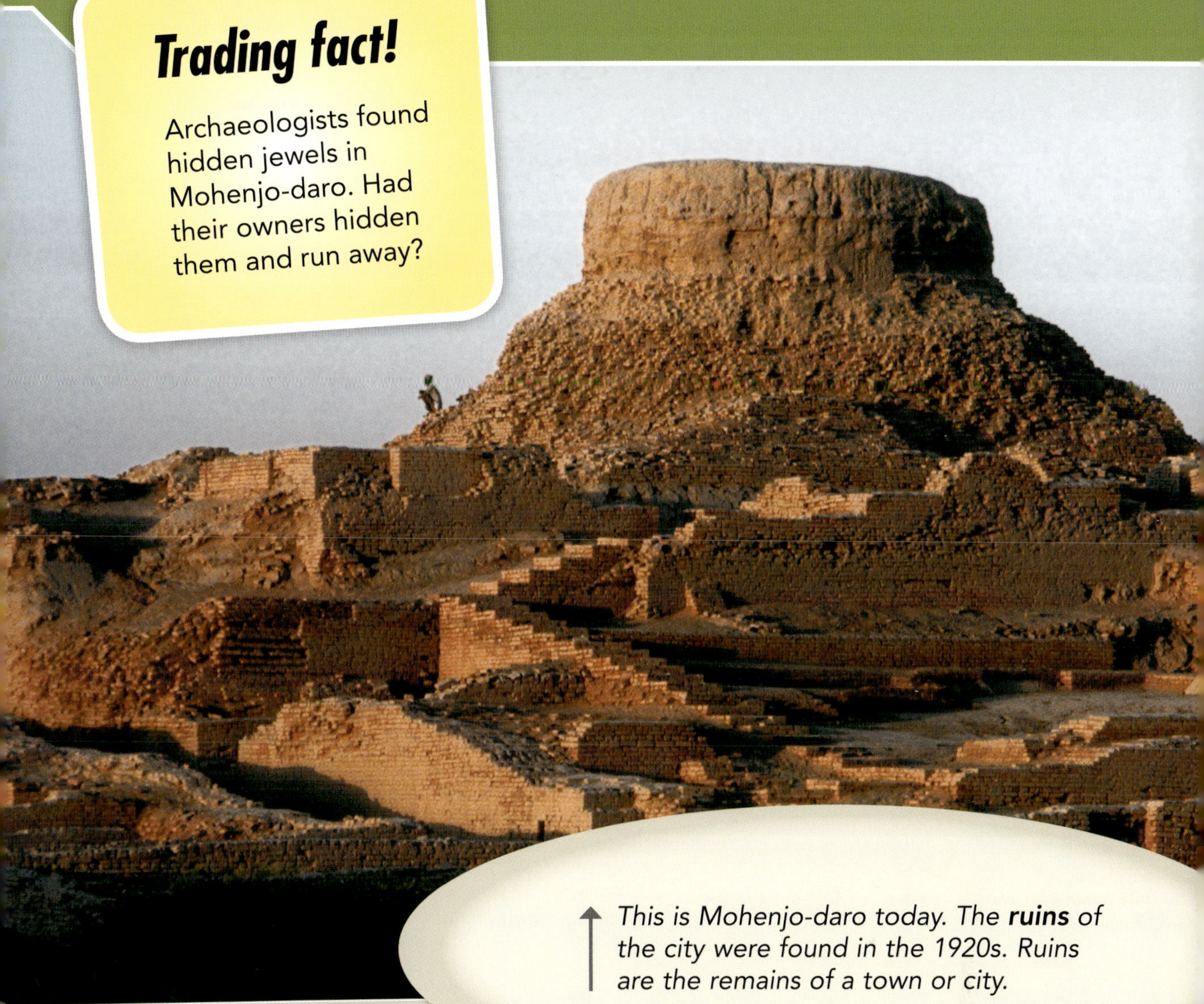

This is Mohenjo-daro today. The ***ruins*** *of the city were found in the 1920s. Ruins are the remains of a town or city.*

It is possible the city dried up. The river may have moved. Without water, people had to move out.

Traders stopped coming to the city. After about 800 years the Indus **civilization** ended. But some of these people's ways lived on in India and Pakistan (see map on page 4).

Fascinating facts!

Experts do not know how many people lived in the Indus Valley. It may be 1 million. It could be 4 million.

Cameras in balloons took pictures of Mohenjo-daro in the 1980s. The pictures showed the city plan.

A girl's skull was found in a jar. The jar was hidden in a wall. Why? Was it to bring luck to a building?

Indus children had lots of toys. They had toy monkeys that slid down strings. Clay bird whistles were used. They also had toy carts.

Rivers do dry up sometimes. The River Sarasvati flowed east of the River Indus. Then it went dry. Many Indus Valley towns were near this river.

Paw prints of cats and dogs have been found in **mud bricks**. Pets ran across the soft mud before it was dry!

Timeline

BC

500,000–100,000
People make stone tools. They use flint (a stone that can be chipped to make it sharp). They hunt animals and collect plants to eat.

5000
People start to be farmers. They plant wheat and grow vegetables. They keep animals such as cows, sheep, and chickens.

The Indus people make clay pots.

2500
People in the Indus Valley are building cities. The biggest cities are now called Harappa, Mohenjo-daro, and Dholavira.

2300–2000
Indus cities are rich and busy. People make beads and metal tools. **Traders** use **seals**. People are good at maths. They can read and write.

2000–1900
Beginning of the end for the Indus **civilization**. People leave big cities, but there is no sign of war.

1900–1700
Bad times for Mohenjo-daro. The city is not kept clean. Building stops.

1700
Mohenjo-daro and other cities are abandoned. People coming from Central Asia in the northwest may have moved in. They may have mixed with the Indus people.

AD

1800s
Explorers find the **ruins** of Harappa.

1920s
Mohenjo-daro is found by Indian **archaeologist** Rakhal Das Banerji.

Glossary

archaeologist person who digs in the ground to find out about the past. Archaeologists found Mohenjo-daro.

ceremony special public acts, such as worship of a god or honouring a ruler. A school assembly is a kind of ceremony.

civilization way of life that is highly developed. Civilized people have many skills.

dung waste made by animals. The Indus people used dung to help colour the pots they made.

funeral ceremony for a dead person. A funeral is a way to say goodbye to a dead person.

goods things people make and sell. Indus people did not use money but simply swapped goods.

hieroglyphics writing of ancient Egypt. Hieroglyphics used pictures instead of words.

Hindu someone who believes in Hinduism. Hinduism is an ancient religion that began in India.

mud brick brick made from wet dirt, often mixed with straw. Mud bricks were used to make buildings.

ox animal of the cattle family, used for pulling ploughs and carts. The plural of ox is oxen.

precious stones stones that are colourful and worth a lot of money. People wear precious stones as jewels.

priest someone who leads people in religious worship. Priests lead the worship in temples.

raw material wood, stone, clay. Raw materials are things we use to make something else.

ruins remains of a building or town. Archaeologists dig in ruins to find clues to the past.

seal kind of stamp. Seals were probably used on trading goods to show who the goods belonged to.

shutters small wooden doors over windows. Shutters kept out sun, wind, rain – and thieves!

statue model of people or animals. Statues can be made from clay, metal, wood, or stone.

taxes money or goods paid to rulers. Indus people paid their taxes in goods.

temple building for religious worship. People go to temples to pray to gods.

trader person who buys and sells things. Traders travelled from place to place to trade.

weapon tool for killing people in war. Weapons were made in workshops.

Want to know more?

Books to read

Indus Valley City, Gillian Clements (Sea to Sea Publications, 2009)

The Indus Valley, Jane Shuter (Heinemann Library, 2007)

Websites

http://www.ancientindia.co.uk/indus/home_set.html
This site from the British Museum has a story about a day in the life of a beadmaker's son.

www.harappa.com
This site has pictures of Harappa and Mohenjo-daro.

http://www.bbc.co.uk/schools/primaryhistory/indus_valley/
On this website you can learn all about life in the Indus Valley.

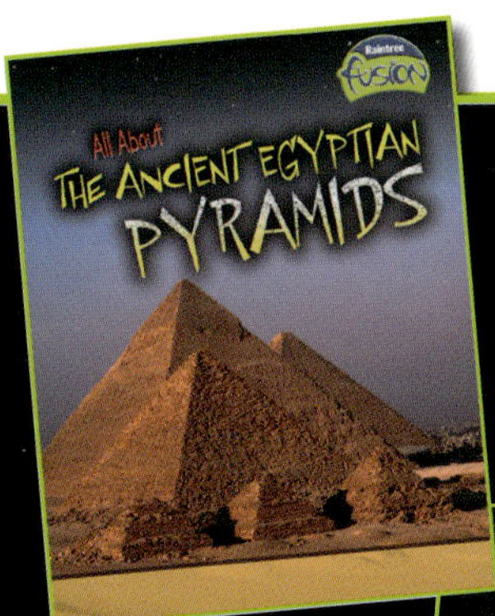

Read about the people who lived in ancient Egypt in ***All About the Ancient Egyptian Pyramids***.

Read about daily life in Roman times in ***All About Life in Ancient Rome***.

Index